I0879146

ABANDONED EASTERN VIRGINIA

FORSAKEN FRAGMENTS OF THE FIRST COLONY

LINDA G. CASSADA

AMERICA THROUGH TIME®
ADDING COLOR TO AMERICAN HISTORY

America Through Time is an imprint of Fonthill Media LLC
www.through-time.com
office@through-time.com

Published by Arcadia Publishing by arrangement with Fonthill Media LLC
For all general information, please contact Arcadia Publishing:
Telephone: 843-853-2070
Fax: 843-853-0044
E-mail: sales@arcadiapublishing.com
For customer service and orders:
Toll-Free 1-888-313-2665

www.arcadiapublishing.com

First published 2019

ISBN 978-1-63499-172-8

Typeset in Trade Gothic 10pt on 15pt
Printed and bound in England

ACKNOWLEDGMENTS

One of my greatest memories from childhood was riding on the back of my father's Honda Gold Wing in the sweltering heat of summer. Though it has been a long time since I've ridden with him, I can close my eyes and feel that occasional sway as he leaned the motorcycle left and right around curves on those backcountry roads. I can hear the twang of Hank Williams songs and the melodic voice of Patsy Cline playing through the speakers. I can smell the sweet and pungent aroma of the honeysuckle growing along the roadsides. But the most powerful and enduring sentiment is that flutter of excitement and joy that I felt when my father's gloved hand would rise to point out an abandoned home to one side of the road.

I was the son that you never had. Your riding partner. Your fishing partner. Your buddy. For these memories and for the opportunity to simply be your daughter, I will forever be grateful. I love you, Daddy.

CONTENTS

ABOUT THE AUTHOR

Since she was young, Linda Cassada has been traversing the backcountry roads of Virginia in search of abandoned places. Now, armed with a BA in professional writing, artistic talent, and a passion for all things mysterious and paranormal, Linda searches for dilapidated structures and forgotten objects. Using words, sketches, and photography, she breathes life into these lost treasures once more, in the hope they will live on in the memories of others as they live on in hers.

Linda's photography can be found on Facebook, Backroad Remnants, as well as on Instagram, @BackroadRemnants.

INTRODUCTION

By human hands, objects are born. We use the objects, love them, and care for them. We imbue them with our energy and bring life to them. Then, we kill them.

Such savages, we are. So careless and wasteful. We move about our busy lives, making, using and discarding. Making more. Using more. Discarding more.

We give not a glance at the large home we pass on the way to work—the one with the rusted tin roof and rotten clapboard siding the color of the sky during a storm. It sits down that dirt lane, watching us through shattered glass panes as we pass, wishing only to be filled with love, the sounds of children's laughter and the smell of supper cooking on the stove.

We care not for the old, rusted chunk of metal with faded red paint that sits nestled in a bed of golden grass where it was parked so long ago. It can barely see over the grass now, watching us scurry about like rats. If only it could feel the heat of its engine burning beneath its hood. What it would give to rumble and roar to life once more before rocketing down the road. But now, everyone wants the shiny, new cars made of plastic—the ones whose engines come to life with the push of a button. No one wants the old chunk of rust. So, there it will remain in its bed of eternal slumber until it sinks into the cold earth and becomes nothing.

And what of that small, broken building with shattered glass windows and a sagging roof, sitting surrounded by slabs of cracked pavement? We pass it as we move about in our plastic, push-button cars, and never do we consider the amount of sugary bliss that it delivered to delighted children across its laminate countertops. Never do we think of that rusty ice cream machine that still lies within, waiting to mix and pour just one more cone for a waiting child with sparkling eyes. Now, its only visitor is a mouse that scampers across the top of it on its way to another place.

Without consideration for anything but ourselves, we've abandoned the countryside and the belongings that were once loved—no, cherished. We want more than what's old, because we believe that what's newer and faster is somehow better, if only because it makes us look better. We plow down the old buildings that were built and inhabited by our ancestors to make room for condos and shopping malls. We seek jobs that pay more because farming and working with our hands won't get us those poorly built homes and plastic, push-button cars that we so desire. And we are so consumed by these desires that we never even pause to consider the birth, the life, and the death of the buildings and objects around us. Somehow people starve, and yet fertile fields sit devoid of crops. People sleep on the streets, and yet homes that would love only to shelter us sit alone and empty.

Such savages, we are ...

This book is a tribute to those things long forgotten—to the abandoned homes built with scarce hardwood timbers and handcrafted bricks, to the cars made of good, American steel that have been left to the will of the harsh elements and to the tools and equipment people once used to make life a bit easier and that brought so much joy to our grandparents and great-grandparents.

This book that you now hold in your hands is proof that there are still a few of us who value the old, the forgotten, the chunks of metal in the fields and the graying homes with holes in the roofs.

1

HOMES

In the minds of many, the word "home" conjures up feelings of comfort and sanctuary, a place where we live and grow and often find refuge from the chaos of day-to-day existence. However, there comes a point when we must either abandon a home or be forced out.

Homes are abandoned for various reasons. Sometimes old age causes us to leave behind all but a few belongings and the memories of life lived there. Sometimes a disaster or poor upkeep makes the home unlivable. And sometimes financial income dwindles and the bank forces the owners out.

No matter the case, each abandoned home we pass impels both curiosity and sadness. It causes us to wonder what brought this structure—once so full of life—to a state of emptiness, loss, and despair.

This abandoned beauty is surrounded by crops and farmland. Occasionally, you can see the man who owns the home and acreage riding his tractor through the fields.

A view from the front shows how the roof has completely caved in, and there is now just a gaping hole where the front door used to be.

Many homes like this one seem as if they should still be lived in. Perhaps it is the beauty of the trees and purple flowers in the front yard that give the home a breath of life.

Alongside a highway in the northeastern part of the state, I spotted this stone house sitting alone and empty. Very few homes in this area are built with stone.

When most homes become abandoned, it seems as if nature slowly creeps in and takes over. With this home, it seems as if nature was living inside and all at once exploded out of the first floor.

The lack of plants and other greenery around this home is what drew me to it. I can imagine a giant lifting the home from where it once stood and placing it gently upon this barren field.

Old House Woods is a tract of dense woods shrouded in mystery and legend. For 200 years people have been telling ghost stories about the place. This is one of the many abandoned houses that sits in or near the woods.

As I drove past this home, I almost didn't see that there was a manmade structure here, seemingly suspended in a state of collapse.

Above: A view of the right side of the home reveals an open doorway. Of course, I had to take a closer look to see what the home may still contain.

Left: Seeing the debris on the floor, it seemed odd that the shelf was still intact, hanging there on the wall as if holding out hope that someone may come along and set a coffee mug on it.

Another interesting find is this sink, which seems in good condition except for the gathering of leaves and sticks in it.

A window hides in a nook formed by two exterior walls, but it's hard to determine if we are on the inside looking out, or the outside looking in.

This beautiful home, with shutters still intact, stands in Mathews County. The interesting thing is that someone didn't care enough to take care of the home, but cared enough about something on the porch to cover it with a tarp.

Opposite above: Another lost treasure of Old House Woods in Mathews County is this farmhouse. Through thickets and underbrush, I had to climb just to get close enough to get this picture. From the road, only the peak of the roof was visible.

Opposite below: At first, I considered this just another sad curiosity, but upon closer inspection, I decided that the bars over the lower windows were the true curiosity.

The above-ground pool behind the home appears to still be in one piece. However, I can only imagine what the water inside it must look like.

I almost didn't spot this home because it blends so well with the woods. The trees, covered with vines, seem to be guarding the home from trespassers.

A single, bare path through amber fields leads to this pristine, abandoned home.

The multiple signs outside warn people that entering the home could be dangerous. The signs may only serve to make us curious enough about what danger lies within.

When this home was last painted, the owner must've chosen from nature's palette. The green shutters and red, rusty roof seem so much a part of the environment that it feels as if this house might've been built by nature itself.

A bit of decorative woodwork at the eaves of the roof still remains, though it has lost its coat of green paint.

This home looks as if it could be facing a lake in the mountains. I can envision the owners sitting on the porch, sipping coffee as ducks float by on a lake that existed only in their minds.

This home took my breath away. Was it a plantation home at one time? It's easy to image horse-drawn carriages pulling up out front to deliver guests to a grand ball.

This home has a moral. You can patch the holes in your life with whatever is lying around, but only the right materials will allow you to endure the harsh elements.

Patch it with the wrong materials, and eventually you will end up as lost and empty as this home.

This home peeps over the thick underbrush at the approaching deer in the foreground.

Alone in the marshes of Gloucester County, this home appears to have pines growing from it.

How did it come to be in this condition? The only explanation was that the home was supported by stilts and that the ones at the rear of the home gave way, causing the entire home to fall backwards.

The yard and weed-free, gravel driveway of this home shows that someone still frequents it. However, unless they are growing plants in the fireplace, it is most certainly abandoned.

I noticed this homestead beside the interstate in north central Virginia. It was difficult to determine how long it had been abandoned.

Numerous outbuildings still stood on the land, some containing hay and other farm equipment.

Every square inch of the floor inside the home was covered with what appeared to be fabric and sawdust. I looked for signs of carpenter bees, but saw none of their telltale, dime-sized holes.

Did the gaping hole in the roof cause the home to be abandoned? Or did the abandonment cause the gaping hole?

This quaint, abandoned home in the marshes of Gloucester County has boarded up windows. However, holes in the roof remain open. A few bushes with red flowers have taken up residence here.

Left: This light green home blends so well with the surrounding foliage that I almost didn't see it.

Below: The Captain Forrest House used to sit in the heart of the notoriously haunted Old House Woods. The house became an icon to thrill seekers and ghost hunters until one fell through the floor and broke his leg. The home was destroyed just a short time after this picture was taken.

Right: The town of Waverly, Virginia, is full of homes such as this one. They are large homes that it seems must've been occupied by a prominent citizen of the town when it was still thriving. Now, as the town dies, it seems to be taking the homes with it.

Below: Perhaps the farmer decided to leave his failing tractors there to keep the home company as it slips back to non-existence.

Illuminated by the setting sun, this home doesn't seem in too bad of a shape. However, the front windows have been boarded and it is obvious that the owner does not intend to return to occupy it.

At first, it was hard to figure out why this home was abandoned. Upon closer inspection I noticed the ridgeline of the roof, sagging toward the right side of the home.

If it weren't for the roof being peeled back like a can of sardines, I would've thought that this home was still lived in.

Which came first: the home or the magnolia tree? The two seem so integrated that I imagine the branches of this grand tree have grown into the back windows of the home and are helping to support the structure.

Someone cared enough to carefully board up the windows. Perhaps this was a family home, too precious to part with, but too old to occupy.

The lavender flowers and bright green foliage make the property seem full of life as the home it hides is slowly fading.

The bright red camper shell, belonging to a truck that is nowhere to be seen, is the reason I spotted this home. At first glance, I couldn't tell whether it was abandoned or not. But the sign on the tree tells the tale.

This large farmhouse hides behind a clump of trees. The chimneys are home to plants and wildlife.

The entrance to a home that no longer exists on Turkey Island in Charles City County was flanked by these stone walls and blocked by an iron gate.

Though it leans and has become entangled with vines, this home stubbornly resists destruction.

Oh, what I would give to get a glimpse inside this grand home! I can almost see the original woodwork—the balustrade, the moldings, the flooring—still intact, but covered with a layer of dust.

It seems so old that even the trees have realized the home will never again be occupied and have decided to accompany the home in its passage away from this world.

Left: A peek inside a window shows that people have been using this home as a garbage dump. I'm sure that while the wildlife appreciates it, the neighbors can probably smell the stench a mile away on a hot summer day.

Below: There are dozens of homes like this one that now sit on property that has been rezoned for commercial use.

2

BARNS AND SHEDS

Outbuildings often escape our focus and attention. They are structures out there in a field, apart from the home, where cats and rodents find shelter. However, these structures often contain fragments of our lives that cannot fit into the home, fragments that can remain long after the home has been abandoned. Barns and sheds can contain treasures from a bygone era, and each one we find abandoned is a beautiful mystery full of curiosity and wonder.

With structures such as this, it is hard to imagine how it could still be standing. One more vulture on the roof and the whole thing could come collapsing down to the ground.

This barn illustrates a lesson that I learned early on in life when hunting for abandoned structures. Birds land on fences and other manmade structures, depositing their seed-filled excrement upon the ground around it and causing trees and bushes to grow. If you want to see an abandoned home, look for a clump of trees.

Within this barn, the treasure was the beauty of the shattered floor joists, covered with moss and dampened by a recent rain.

The triangular peak of a roof is often what helps me to spot a structure within the trees and underbrush.

This patchwork piece of history, kissed by the setting sun, is perhaps the most beautiful barn that I have ever seen.

Opposite above: Someone took great care in creating the masonry siding of the home and garage. Now, the contents of the garage that were left behind seem to be attempting a slow escape from certain death.

Opposite below: Hues of red, green, and yellow are the perfect contrast to the greyish tones of this barn sitting beside a road in Gloucester County.

Above: I am convinced that this owner was determined to have a shed, but lacked the proper materials to build one. He collected whatever he could find to make the shed, and now, a portion of the metal roof juts up as if to wave at those passing by.

Left: Streaks of white upon the emerald siding seem like strips of white frostings dripping down the sides of a Mother Nature's gingerbread house. What those white strips truly are, and how they have remained so white, is a mystery.

Like the subject of a Dali painting, this barn appears to be slowly melting.

A double-bay barn sits out in a field in Surry County. The untended fields around it and the vines beginning to grow over it are a sure sign that it has been left to rot.

An old barn with a hay loft begins its descent from existence.

3

COMMERCIAL LOCATIONS

Commercial structures are our home away from home. They not only serve as a source of income for many, but they often contain the products that make life possible. However, much like homes, commercial structures can also become abandoned. Owners will leave behind products, signs, and crates that elude to the business's purpose. They can be fascinating and wonderous places where we are compelled to find a broken window and peek through, so we can catch a glimpse of what may have been left behind.

N. S. BOYKIN
DRYER

Fort Monroe was decommissioned in 2011 and currently is being sold off in pieces to private citizens. Many concrete structures such as this one still stand around the haunted fort.

Opposite above: That's a big dryer. It's easy to infer that because this building is located in the cotton and peanut region, it was used to dry one of those crops.

Opposite below: The Hunt Store is one of the few historic, commercial buildings left in the town of Poquoson. Efforts to move and restore the building are currently underway before the building is gone forever.

The general store in Surry County is still in marvelous condition considering its age. It stands on a desolate street corner in the middle of the countryside.

An old gas pump stands to the right of the general store as a tribute to a bygone era.

The oldest section of the general store is this building on the right. It sits directly behind the primary building and boasts an old-fashioned water pump between its doors.

The roof of this old service station fell apart long ago, leaving only the rusted framework. With the concrete block fairly clean for its age, it seems as if the metal roofing was painted red to contrast with the bone white blocks.

This old store, with its wood siding beginning to disintegrate, still has its picture windows. At least the mini blinds in one of the windows are still intact.

Sagging and growing foliage on the roof, it seems that it won't be long before this beautiful old structure is too far gone to be restored.

All that remains of this old church is the brick walls and a graveyard. The arched doorways were built strong enough to withstand the test of time.

Another view of the church walls shows the piles of bricks and the bright green grass growing inside of it.

A bit of the graveyard can be seen through the doorway.

This old building in the town of Poquoson catches my eye every time I pass it. With the vines growing over the concrete block and the short door on the right, the building always intrigues me.

This old building with a unique entrance sits alone beside a highway. It seems that someone was taking care of it at one time. Now, it sits empty, waiting for someone else to come along and fall in love with it as I did.

This old building in the town of Signpine has seen better days. It may have been used as the post office at one time, but also could've been occupied by other merchants, judging from the multiple doors along the front.

It seems that a little bit of the Old West found its way to Gloucester County. This little building seems so out of place, and yet so a part of its surroundings.

The words "Hasty" and "Mart" are all that I can make out of the lettering on the front of this old building. It's obvious that it hasn't been used for anything in a very long time.

Rosewell, the home of the Page family in Gloucester County, used to be one of the grandest plantation homes in the American colonies. Construction was started in 1725, and the home was built to rival the recently built Governor's Palace in Williamsburg. The home burned in 1916, leaving behind only these ruins.

Opposite above: The wine cellar of Rosewell was the setting for a great mystery. During a ball, a slave escaped and fled to the nearby fields. He was quickly captured and returned, then locked in the wine cellar until he could be dealt with in the morning. During the night, the family was awakened by his cries and screams and by the sound of bottles breaking. Thinking that he was simply acting out, they ignored him. However, in the morning when they unlocked the cellar door, they found him dead among a multitude of broken bottles. The manner of death could not be determined. Now, his spirit is said to roam the grounds of the old plantation.

Opposite below: An old train station, barely visible from the road, is all that remains of the railway that used to run through this area. The tracks were torn up long ago. Now, the dilapidated station with its pristine roof sits here waiting for a train that will never arrive.

Another beautiful structure in the town of Waverly is this building that appears to have been used as a school. The lower windows are boarded up and many of the upper windows have been broken.

The arched window over the double doors is one of the few windows still intact.

A view of the upper floor at the back of the building shows damage to the roofline and the vines that have begun to infiltrate the structure.

A quick peek inside one of the lower windows shows shelving with white, porcelain cups and dishes.

Above: A storefront on a lonely corner in the countryside is almost completely obscured by greenery. The aqua blue of the remaining paint and the reddish tones of the wood used to board the windows and door are a stunning match.

Right: Inside the old store, remnants of the store's wares can still be seen sitting on the counter.

NEW DESIGN
SCHOOL
RESTORATION
AFRICAN AMERICAN
HERITAGE SOCIETY

Hints of both wood and brick used in the walls are visible beneath the greenery.

Opposite above: The New Design School was a school for African Americans. The quaint little building is missing its steps and window glass. However, a sign in front shows that it is being restored and will not be lost in history.

Opposite below: This structure is so grown over by foliage that I can no longer tell what the building used to be.

An old church with its steeple still standing tall above the surrounding trees sits nestled into the landscape in Gloucester County. Such a marvelous structure shouldn't go unappreciated.

These buildings are so overgrown that it's hard to tell what they once were. The twin peaks of their roofs jut out above the foliage like a hand waving at me to tell me that they're still here.

Another old structure in Fort Monroe has iron bars at the entrance. A bush devoid of leaves grows just before the gate as if to block people from trying to get in.

The remnants of an old ice cream parlor still stand along the Route 17. The roof of the building is failing, but the window glass remains unbroken.

Inside, a pile of plastic containers covers the floor and the three remaining chairs.

A piece of machinery that may have delivered ice cream to hundreds of smiling children now sits alone inside, rusting away in the midday sun.

A view inside an old building shows the shiplap and plaster that used to cover the walls. The flooring has given in, revealing the ground beneath it.

An old service station sits on a desolate corner in the middle of nowhere. The siding has greyed over time, but the brick bases of the columns remain in good condition.

Another view of the structure shows the failing framework and a definite lean that will eventually lead to destruction.

Eastern State Hospital in Williamsburg is the oldest hospital for the mentally ill in the country. When the original building burned down, the campus was relocated. This is one of the oldest buildings that remains.

The hospital currently houses the criminally insane in a new facility, but a few of these structures from the 1800s still dot the campus. Strange and unexplained lights are seen inside the building at night by the maintenance workers and security guards driving past.

This large building sits along Page Road in Gloucester. The canary yellow paint has worn away and windows have broken.

A different perspective shows the true size of the building. It could've been used as a hotel at one time, and if someone were to decide to fix it up, it would have plenty of room to house a bed and breakfast.

An old department store, now abandoned but occasionally used for a Halloween store, sits in a strip mall among other small stores. During one Halloween, employees of the store that occupied the large, creepy building complained that they were seeing shadows, hearing voices, and feeling the icy touch of an unseen hand.

4

VEHICLES AND FARM EQUIPMENT

Like metal dinosaurs, older vehicles and farm equipment were often made of steel and other materials that would allow them to outlast their owners. So when we pass one lying out in a field, almost obscured by tall grasses, it makes us wonder why it was left there to rot. Was engine trouble what caused it to be abandoned? Did the owner park it, intending to return to it the following day, but never did? Unlike homes and other structures, the reasons for abandoning vehicles and farm equipment seem more elusive. However, this seems to amplify the mystery surrounding them.

An old tractor, missing parts and with a broken front wheel, sits in a field. Could it be that an elderly man was mowing the grass when it broke down, and he hadn't the means to push it back home?

This boat has been there for years and birds like the one seen standing on top have found it a good place to rest.

Old cars are always fascinating. The round headlights, the chrome, even the shapely design of them is such a stark contrast to the vehicles you find today.

Opposite above: Another old tractor that appears intact but for a heavy coating of rust sits among other pieces of equipment in Surry County.

Opposite below: An old truck, buried in shrubs and vines, has found a final resting place near a park in Poquoson. The cab is so covered that it can barely be seen.

Another vehicle, still in good shape, sits in a junkyard among other older vehicles that don't look so good.

A peek inside reveals exactly what is expected. The fabrics are torn and stained. The plastics are faded and cracked.

If I was a farmer, I might be able to identify what all this stuff is. Various pieces of equipment dot a green field. All of it rusts and rots as time continues to pass with only the wildlife finding use for it.

Tucked into the trees and bushes at a park in the city of Hampton, this old piece of farm equipment has seen better days. However, the bright label on the side of it that says to be careful is in surprisingly good condition.

Another tractor, this one covered in vines and stuffed with pine needles, sits on a farm with a few other pieces of equipment.

At an abandoned house, an old tractor and storage shed sit in the side yard with other unidentifiable items. Judging from the items sitting around, I'm sure that the shed is full of lost treasures as well.

A heap of rusted metal, entangled in the greenery, sits at the edge of a field. Pulleys, chains, and a radiator are the most identifiable parts.

A few relics of the Civil War sit at the edge of a battlefield. The wheels, which were once a bright yellow, have faded and have begun to rot.

A single tree, dead but still standing, sits at the edge of a farmer's field. A rusted piece of equipment, barely visible, sits in front of it.

5

OBJECTS

The things we carry, the things we keep: these bits of our lives are used and loved, until they cannot be used any longer. Then they are left to the torment of time. They rust and deteriorate until there is nothing left.

These objects fill abandoned homes, barns and sheds, and commercial locations. They sit alone in the woods and in fields across America, waiting for someone like you and I to discover them and put them to use once again.

An old ammo box sits among brick and other items behind a home. The box could've once contained military ammo. Now, it only contains cobwebs and dust.

A barrel of some sort, covered with dead vines, has been left beside the road. What it might've contained is anyone's guess.

Slabtown was the name of an African American settlement established by the Union army on the outskirts of Yorktown. However, when the National Park Service forced the residents out to form the national park in Yorktown, the previous owners left behind hundreds of relics such as this old bottle.

An antique fan, collecting dust in someone's basement, probably still works. They don't make things like they used to.

An old mailbox, lying along the roadside, will never again hold mail. The wood post that used to support it has rotten away, much like the house the mailbox belonged to.

In the forest beside an old graveyard, this lamb lies in the dirt and mud, most likely blown off a child's grave by a windstorm.

TEXACO
T

I'm not sure why anyone would be digging along the roadside in the marshes of Mathews County, but it they do, they may encounter the underground telephone lines that are likely as abandoned as the sign itself.

Opposite page: An old sign is the only indication that a gas station used to stand beside the road.

A collection of rusted tools, covered in bird excrement, hang on the wall in a shed.

This antique cash register collects dust and grime in a storage shed. I wonder what the primary user of this machine would think if he or she saw the cash registers we have today.

GALLONS
FOR USE AS A
MOTOR FUEL ONLY
CONTAINS
LEAD
(TETRAETHYL)

This Barbie doll lies lifeless and muddy in the basement of a historic home.

Opposite page: A couple of rusted gas pumps, forever frozen in time, sit in the dirt and grass. Vehicles will never again frequent the pumps to fill up for a Sunday drive.

Left: Another old gas pump, still in decent condition, sits in a storage shed full of other forgotten items.

Below: A crumpled piece of unidentifiable material sits on the porch of an abandoned home. I'm forced to wonder what it is and how it came to be left there.

An old metal chair, once green and then painted red, looks like a piece of modern art as it sits on the porch of an abandoned home in Mathews County. A box containing a jar of peanut butter sits next to it. Curiosity wasn't enough to make me open the jar and look inside.

Above: An abandoned Christmas decoration sits in the yard of an abandoned home east of Richmond. He continues to smile, unaware that he may lie in the wet leaves forever.

Opposite page: Horlick's Malted Milk is what this abandoned glass jar used to contain. The jar dates back to the 1930s, and while plants have begun to grow inside of it, the glass has remained intact.

A collection of abandoned netting and crab pots sits in the woods behind an old home.

A water fountain, attached to the side of an abandoned building, collects rain and bits of wood. Like everything else in this book, it served a purpose for a time and will decay until it is forgotten forever.